P9-DGV-068

THE
STRESS-FREE
TRAVELER

Simple Exercises and Stretches to Keep Your Cool on Planes, Trains, and Automobiles

SANDY PATON

Illustrations by Lonni Sue Johnson

McGraw·Hill

New York Chicago San Francisco Lisbon London Madrid Mexico City
Milan New Delhi San Juan Seoul Singapore Sydney Toronto

The **McGraw·Hill** Companies

Library of Congress Cataloging-in-Publication Data

Paton, Sandy, 1946–
    The stress-free traveler : simple exercises and stretches to keep your cool on planes, trains, and automobiles / Sandy Paton ; illustrations by Lonni Sue Johnson.
        p.   cm.
    ISBN 0-07-145605-8 (alk. paper)
    1. Travel—Health aspects.   2. Transportation—Health aspects.
3. Exercise.   4. Stretching exercises.   5. Stress management.   I. Title.

RA783.5.P38   2005
613.6'8—dc22   2005003492

2 3 4 5 6 7 8 9 0   FGR/FGR   0 9 8 7 6 5

ISBN 0-07-145605-8

Interior design by Monica Baziuk
Interior artwork by Lonni Sue Johnson

McGraw-Hill books are available at special quantity discounts to use as premiums and sales promotions, or for use in corporate training programs. For more information, please write to the Director of Special Sales, Professional Publishing, McGraw-Hill, Two Penn Plaza, New York, NY 10121-2298. Or contact your local bookstore.

This book is printed on acid-free paper.

THIS BOOK IS DEDICATED
IN LOVING MEMORY OF SIRI SINGH
SAHIB BHAI SAHIB HARBHAJAN SINGH
KHALSA YOGIJI (AKA, YOGI BHAJAN)
WITHOUT WHOSE TEACHINGS, INSPIRATION,
AND CONTINUAL GUIDANCE THIS WORK
WOULD NOT HAVE BEEN POSSIBLE.

Contents

Acknowledgments

Blessings and thanks to **Swami Sada Shiva Tirtha**, for his undying encouragement to "keep up the energy"; Mahan Rishi Singh Khalsa, for being an inspirational teacher; students Joe Abbey, Rose Ananthanayagam, Jerry Gibson, Sheila Kohler, and Bob Marker, who taught me more than I ever dreamed; Isaiah Davis Jr., terminal manager for Greyhound Lines, Inc., for giving us permission to try these exercises on one of his buses; Cleon O. Williams, driver for Greyhound Lines, who operated our bus and couldn't wait to see his name in print; Eastwind Airlines, for allowing us to board a plane on the runway at West Trenton Airport for a photo shoot; Marriott Hotels, for allowing us the use of a room for a photo shoot; Linda Parks, for her time and talent; Cheryl Boyce—sister, friend, and neighbor—for being an important catalyst; Ravi Singh, for his unstinting support; Mike Valentino, friend and agent; Lonni Sue for saying *yes* to this project and for making it a magical experience; and Lorenzo da Ponte, faithful heroic poodle-puppy-doodle who monitored all of my classes, nurtured and loved all of my students, and never left my side as I wrote.

SANDY PATON

Thank you to Sandy, for her imagination and writing spirit, and for finding a home for this book, and especially for asking me to do drawings! Thanks for all of the chances I've had to travel in beautiful landscapes—far away in jets, ships, trains, buses, and taxis, and close by in little airplanes—all making me appreciate these exercises. And thanks to EB the Siamese and Flo the tabby, who were good company and kept off the drawing table and out of the India ink and watercolor (most of the time); and to the forty-seven cows, five pigs, and one horse who got out and required chasing only two or three times during deadlines; and to the six barn cats who made me laugh with their antics as I walked out to the studio in the barn to draw.

LONNI SUE JOHNSON

Thanks to Meg Leder and John Aherne, superb editors, for seeing the merit in this book; and to the rest of the McGraw-Hill team: Monica Baziuk, Marisa L'Heureux, La Shae Ortiz, Heather Taylor, and Ellen Vinz, who kept everything together. What a blessing!

SANDY PATON AND LONNI SUE JOHNSON

Introduction

Does traveling exhaust you? **Does it give you motion sickness, headaches, backaches, or sore feet?** Do you sometimes pack unresolved emotions along with your clothing or business notes? Does getting to the airport or train or bus station take what's left of you before your journey even begins?

The Stress-Free Traveler is for anyone who dreads getting on a plane, gets carsick on long road trips, or feels claustrophobic on trains. In this book, you'll find a series of exercises to revive and repair you as you travel—or, if you prefer, when you arrive. The exercises have been chosen to accommodate passengers traveling in restricted spaces, such as economy-class airline seats, trains, automobiles, and buses. (They've all been tested en route!) But the exercises can also be practiced anywhere: at home, back at the hotel, or in the conference room.

With the exercises in this book, you'll be able to sit back, relax, and enjoy the trip. In the famous words of Uncle Jed Clampett, the mountaineer oil baron immortalized in "The Beverly Hillbillies," "Take yo' shoes off. Set a spell."

Why I Wrote This Book

A leisurely drive on Route 1, post–rush hour. A good time to travel. No traffic; just the way it should be. I had left the house with nearly half an hour to spare—plenty of time to reach the most convenient airport shuttle, the Airporter. I settled down for my ten-mile drive, feeling invincible. I could have been a Girl Scout after all: always prepared.

But then, much to my horror, there appeared diversion cones, construction crews, red brake lights, and irregular rows of cars. If I didn't know better, I would have supposed this to be traffic! I knew I couldn't miss the Airporter. That would mean driving all the way to the airport and having to find a spot in Long-Term Parking Lot D (*D* for distant) or Lot E (*E* for exile).

I forged ahead, hoping the folks who ran the Airporter would make allowances for the Route 1 construction. After all, I had a reservation. I could hear it now: "Hank, give it another five minutes, we're waiting for a few more passengers. Must be stuck in that mess out on Route 1." Dream on, happy driver.

I did get there, but just in time to see the Airporter leave the hotel parking lot. Undaunted, I parked my car, grabbed my attaché case, and ran like the wind. So long as the van was in sight, there was hope. And there it was! A signal from the driver: he would make the turn on Route 1 and come back for me.

As I got on the Airporter, I took as many long, deep breaths as I could to settle down. I thanked the driver profusely and remarked about the awful traffic on Route 1, but I was curtly reminded, "The Airporter leaves at 10:20, lady, not a minute later—period." So I sat down, careful not to make eye contact with anyone. I was aware of sighs and nervous glances at wristwatches. I could hear fingers punching out work on laptops, calls being made on cellular phones, and urgent messages being breathlessly recorded onto handheld recorders. We all could have used a dose or two of relaxation.

Travel—whether it's the daily commute, the vacation trip, or the urgent business trip—exacts a

toll. When we compound the physical punishment of rushing to trains, planes, and buses or elbowing for the next taxi or a spot (not a seat) on the subway with ticketing, checking luggage, and being checked ourselves, we aren't challenging our bodies—we're punishing them. How prepared for meetings and vacations can we be when we can't even take a moment to step back from it all?

I teach Kundalini yoga, a transformational type of yoga that can enable you to experience "infinity in the finite." Kundalini yoga combines breathing, movement, meditation, stretching, and relaxation techniques in a way that is accessible to everyone—at every level and almost any age. Fantastic stuff. I decided to write this book because I like to teach yoga, and I have something wonderful to share. If I can repair just one person's nervous system, I will have a successful project. What have you got to lose, except maybe the twitch in your right eye, your gastritis, your colitis, your palpitations, your TMJ, or that familiar cold sweat? Unless you're wedded to these earthly sensations, read on. Put your notepads and pens and desktop contraptions down. Unclench your fists and your teeth. Unbutton your collar; slip off your shoes. This time's for you.

How to Use This Book

One of the benefits of yoga is to make you flexible, so I structured this book with that in mind. Be flexible. Choose a chapter you think best suits your current need and follow the exercises in the order they are recommended. You will notice that some exercises should be practiced in sequence; others can be mixed and matched. Some of the exercises are preparatory. Consequently, they might be repeated in several chapters to help you loosen up and get the kinks out. Any exercise that stands alone (for example, the relaxation exercises in

Chapter 1) should be practiced only for the number of minutes recommended. But if a stand-alone exercise appeals to you or seems to work particularly well for you, you may increase the time gradually in increments of two to three minutes a session until you can practice an exercise for thirty-one to sixty-two minutes. Remember, there is no magic to the amount of time you practice an exercise; however, the longer you can do one without distractions, the better. Pick and choose the stand-alone exercises and chapters that appeal to you. There is only one caveat: have fun.

Preparing for the Exercises

The exercise sets in this book were designed to accommodate the limited range of movement you have when you travel and to help you overcome that cramped feeling. If the passengers around you are put off as you go through the exercises, ask them to join you. Either they will join you or will oblige you by moving to other seats, giving you still more room to move around. You can't lose.

As you move through the exercises in this book, keep the following guidelines in mind:

➤ Sit with your spine straight. For most of the exercises, your vertebrae should be aligned perfectly to allow the energy to flow from the base of your spine to your crown (the top of your head).

➤ Keep both feet flat on the floor. This helps to ground you and keep your hips aligned. If your feet or legs are crossed, your hips will not be perfectly aligned and pressure will be unevenly distributed.

➤ Close your eyes (unless otherwise indicated) to focus your attention solely on your body and your feelings. Closing your eyes will block out light and other distractions and help you concentrate on your breathing and your movements.

➤ Fix your eyes on the space between your brows (unless otherwise indicated). Raising your eyes to this point might feel a little strange at first, but it is very effective on several levels. It will help to focus your mind and will stretch and strengthen your ocular muscles. Longtime practitioners of yoga will also tell you that this is a tool for seeing things clearly—in other words, it hones your intuitive abilities.

➤ Keep your head straight and chin tucked slightly. If your head is not aligned with your spine, this can create a physical block that will prevent your energy from rising unimpeded.

➤ Relax your jaw, brow, and tongue. Ever notice when your tongue is plastered to the roof of your mouth? Sometimes we forget that even these parts of our face and head need to be relaxed, too.

➤ Relax your shoulders; try not to hunch them. I can't tell you how many times I have had to shake someone's shoulders down. Look around at the people in the airport or at work. Check out how many shoulders are hunched and how many shoulders are well

aligned. It will give you a clue to what's going on in their guts, too.

➤ Rest your hands gently on your knees or thighs. It is best to keep books and other things off your lap while you do the exercises.

➤ Rest for at least a minute between exercises. This allows the energy of the previous movements to take effect.

➤ Take liberal draughts of water (preferably spring water) from time to time. Travel and stress both deplete water from your tissues. In addition, your muscles and tissues will demand more water as you do the exercises.

➤ Gradually increase the length of time you practice each exercise until you can manage the recommended times. These exercises are very powerful; they both ground you and raise your energy. Consequently, they require practice. Lengthen your practice time as you become more comfortable with the exercises.

➤ Move at a pace that suits you. It is best to go slowly and cautiously at first. Let's face it, if you have just completed a mini-marathon while lugging a suitcase—wheels or no wheels—to the baggage check, you need time to regroup. Take it easy. That's what these exercises are all about. You need to allow your body to become accustomed to the positions. Racing through the exercises will defeat their purpose and could cause injury as you make demands on already compromised muscles. Make each movement a meditation.

➤ Do not force yourself through an exercise. Do your best. If you cannot complete an exercise or you cannot move fully as directed, don't punish yourself. Do what you can.

Note: If you have a heart condition, you should consult your physician before attempting any of these exercises.

Breathe

Along with the points noted above, you'll also need to focus on your breathing as you move through the exercises. When you close your eyes and become comfortable with the movements in an exercise, attempt to focus on your breath. The idea is to get to a point where you can block out all other sounds and hear only your breathing.

It is also important to breathe properly. Somehow on the way to adulthood, we begin to lose the ability to cry, laugh, and breathe with abandon. Our breath becomes shallow; our chest and vocal cords become taut. To practice these exercises, you'll need to return to your earlier breathing patterns. Take a lesson from a baby. When a baby cries or laughs, his belly moves—the original "bowl-full-of-jelly" laugh, the one they credit to Santa Claus. Breathe like a baby: from your abdomen, not from your chest.

As you breathe, relax your abdomen; allow it to expand as you inhale. When you exhale, bring your navel to your spine and push the air out. Squeeze your abdomen further in, and you will find there is still more air to expel. Do you remember being punched in the belly when you were a kid? When that happened, the air was forcefully expelled from your lungs. Well, that's what you want to do—only in slow motion. Squeeze the air out from your abdomen. Relax your belly on the inhale; bring it to your spine on the exhale. Don't raise your shoulders as you inhale; most people tend to do that. Relax your shoulders and breathe into your abdomen. A strong breath requires the full support of your diaphragm.

Yogic tradition teaches that increased lung capacity alters your personality. In fact, the length of breath is directly related to your ability to see things more clearly. Breathing slowly, taking three or four breaths per minute, is ideal. The longer, slower, and deeper your breathing, the better you will be able to manage daily crises with aplomb. Can you imagine yourself calmer, more collected, more able to carry on with dignity and grace? Next time you're really angry or upset, take several long pulls on the air, keeping your chest, shoulders, and facial muscles relaxed. Then check your mood. If you are still angry or upset, breathe still more deeply.

Remember, you were born with your own home nerve repair kit: your lungs. Breathe consciously today. Bet you anything that as you prepared to catch this plane or train or whatever conveyance you are on, you barely noticed your breathing until suddenly you were out of breath. Eh? Next time you are standing in an elevator or on an escalator or one of those moving walkways at the airport, or even while you are waiting for the plane at Gate B22, become aware of your breath and attempt to breathe long and deeply. Go ahead. It will feel delicious.

Quiet for the Wandering Mind

Along with practicing deep belly breathing, it's helpful to clear your mind as you engage in the exercises. This can be especially challenging when you're surrounded by traffic and frantic fellow travelers. You might be wondering if you've packed your toothbrush and deodorant, or if you brought the files your boss asked you to carry, or if you are to meet the client in the hotel lobby or at the convention center, or even if you remembered to fill the gas tank of the airport rental car. Let these distracting thoughts go. Think of nothing but the movements of the exercise. Keep in mind that when you attempt to clear one thought, you'll notice that many more often emerge. In order to stop the mental patter, don't stop to examine your thoughts. Allow them to go by.

If you're still having a hard time, try repeating (either aloud or in your head) a word or words to correspond with the rhythm of your breath. (This might help to muffle the cries from the baby several seats ahead.) Some people choose numbers, such as one-two-three-four: inhaling on one, exhaling on two, and so on. Others may choose words. You can, for example, inhale on "bliss" and exhale on "bounty." Any prayer, name, or word that is special to you can help you through a stressful situation and bring you to a peaceful state. I know someone who softly repeats "puppy," a word with gentle and playful connotations. In Gurmukhi (a language that predates Punjabi), there is a beauti-

ful mantra, Sat Nam (pro-
nounced "sut nahm"), meaning
true name or true identity,
addressing the immutable core of
your being. The object of repeating
a mantra is to keep the mental
patter from becoming men-
tal clatter. Choose a simple word or phrase that
will help comfort and
heal your frazzled mind and body and keep your
mind off things that are not within your control at
the moment.

You might find that even though you have iden-
tified your word or phrase, the mind will fight all
the harder for recognition. However, it can be useful to learn (but not cling to) what is coming to the
fore as you attempt to sit peacefully. And it is
important to know that this is all a part of the pro-
cess of clearing. Seeking praise, one student
remarked to his teacher that when he sat quietly
with his eyes closed for several minutes, he saw
beautiful temples and great works of art. His
teacher merely smiled and dismissed his experi-

ence, saying, "These distractions too shall pass." The idea is to eliminate distracting thought altogether. Empty your mind. Be in the moment. Concentrating on your breath and your word or mantra will help you do this. Presumably, you can be no other place than you are now, even if you are waiting for a delayed flight and even if you have missed the all-important presentation. Be in the moment. You will be surprised at what you might find!

Packing for the Journey

There are some simple travel accessories you should pack for your journey. In short, remember things that will make your life easier: a sweater or sweatshirt for the plane; your comfy slippers for a long flight; water; and moist towelettes. Don't underestimate their importance. If you are chilly or thirsty or get something sticky on your hands, your travel experience will be less enjoyable and the effect of these exercises will be compromised. Do yourself a favor: pack all the stuff that you think you would like to have with you. Most suitcases have wheels. (And if you don't have one with wheels, it's time to get one!) Lug your stuff along. This is all about feeling good away from home.

Water

Never deny yourself that cool drink of water. You have heard that the human body is 70 percent water. And you have probably also heard that the human body requires eight eight-ounce glasses of water per day. Insufficient hydration will dehydrate your muscles, your tissues, and your organs, including your skin and your brain. Dehydration can cause constipation, fatigue, indigestion, and a host of other problems. Without water, the electrical charges in your body will diminish. Without sufficient water, homeostasis cannot be maintained and your body's physiological responses will diminish. Water carries waste from the body and helps you maintain a normal temperature.

Remember: for every hour in an airplane, you will lose two pints of water through dehydration. Add to that the amount of water you lost from running to the plane or during last-minute packing. If you don't drink while you travel, you will become dehydrated.

The exercises in this book will heighten your sensitivity to your body. And if you attempt these exercises without sufficient hydration, you will likely become acutely and uncomfortably aware of your body's distress. So drink up! Keep a fresh container of water in your car or your carry-on at all times.

Spray Bottle

Traveling—particularly on airplanes—can dry your skin as well as your throat. Pack a spray bottle

filled with spring water.
If you are lucky
enough to have
a garden in
bloom (or
a florist
nearby),
add a few
flower petals to
the water. Set the bottle in the sun for a few minutes, and you will have made your own floral
spritzer. Or you can squeeze a few drops of fresh
lemon juice into the spritzer. Remember to refresh
and spritz your neck and face from time to time.
This will not only help keep you cool, but will
refresh you.

Moist Towelettes

Take my word for it. Whether you use them for a
quick clean-up after the airline snack, to renew the
color in your cheeks, or to wipe your hands after
checking the dipstick in your rental car, you'll be
grateful that you packed them.

Salt

After an extended journey in stale, oxygen-poor air, it is essential to draw impurities from your skin. When you finally reach your destination, take a refreshing bath in kosher salt or Dead Sea salts (available in health food stores). Add a cup or two to your bath; allow it to dissolve, then hop in and relax. Even after a day trip, I sometimes prepare a gala salt bath at home with lights out, scented candles flickering, and my favorite tape on the portable deck. Sponge off as usual after your salt cleansing.

In a warm climate (or in warm weather), you might want to end your shower with cool water. This will tighten your skin, minimize your pores, and enhance your circulation. It will also help to rinse all of the shampoo out of your hair and all the soap off your body. Afterward, vigorously rub your skin with a towel and gently massage a small amount of almond oil into your skin (see Chapter 7). Look for high-quality massage oils. First cold-pressed virgin oil is the best. It means that the oils used were extracted from the first pressing. An oil labeled "virgin" indicates that it is filtered naturally without chemical treatment or refining, so it is rich in natural nutrients. Look for oils that are fresh-smelling, bottled in dark bottles (avoid clear glass bottles), and certified organic, if possible.

Food

I found, quite by accident, that the less I ate before or while traveling, the better off I was. However, after experimenting with several diets on numerous trips, I found the perfect meal for the road: macrobiotic food. No, I don't follow this diet daily, but I do pack containers of macrobiotic foods specifically for long flights. The trick is to avoid oils, salt, and anything processed, smoked, or fried. Check around; find someone local who makes macrobiotic meals.

If this is all too much for you, pack a simple meal and carry it on. Anything that you make will be many times better for your system than something somebody else has made. In short, before you travel and while you travel, eat less: less fat, less salt, less sugar, fewer processed foods, no alcohol, and no caffeine. Above all, avoid eating before you attempt the exercises in this book, or allow at least two hours before you do. They are best performed on an empty stomach.

Remedies for Motion Sickness

Motion sickness occurs when the vestibular apparatus of the ears, eyes, and senses sends conflicting messages to your brain. The best way to deal with motion sickness is to prevent it. Patches and med ications and even some herbal remedies for motion sickness are available in many pharmacies and health food stores. If you find yourself in a health food store before your next trip, you might want to pick up some charcoal tablets. The charcoal detox ifies your system, particularly the liver. Take as directed, usually one hour before your trip.

Ginger, either in capsules or candied, is another useful and tasty remedy. It's great for digestion and a wonderful remedy for an upset stomach. It also helps prevent nausea caused by motion sickness. Ginger tea—now available in many supermarkets—might provide a nice change of pace from caffeinated drinks.

If you are prone to nausea, you might also want to try taking vitamin B_6 (pyridoxine), which might help relieve it. Take 100 milligrams one hour before your trip and another 100 milligrams two hours after your trip. Also try wearing special wristbands created for preventing motion sickness—they work by putting pressure on specific points on the wrist. The wristbands alone might not provide sufficient relief, so check out several remedies before you fly. Most important, do not eat before you fly, and politely refuse the airline snacks. Better to arrive hungry than ill.

One More Tip for the Road

Students sometimes try to perfect hand positions or postures to such a degree that they miss the point. Just do your best. If you can only reach your thighs when you are asked to reach your knees, you are already doing your best. If you can only do one minute and not the prescribed two or three or more, you are doing your best. Be aware of how you accept the directions in the book. If you become tense as you attempt to perfect them, stop! Listen to your body and start again. Your reaction might provide a clue as to how you respond to other directives or suggestions.

Besides, there is nothing magical about doing all of the movements perfectly for the maximum amount of time. Work your way there and beyond gradually, while listening to your body. If you are comfortable, then do more. If you are tight and unable to do an exercise, choose another. If you need to modify an exercise, by all means modify it until you can achieve the correct posture. There is no prize for achieving a "perfect score." Remember, the objective is to relieve stress, not cause more of it. Go ahead and be like a kid in a candy shop. Have fun shopping; try what appeals to you or what your body is screaming for.

Whether you're on the commuter flight from New York to Boston, or on your way to Turkey or Tokyo, devote time to yourself. If you are determined to catch up on work during the trip, prepare for the work (and later recuperate from it) with the exercises in the following chapters. If you're on vacation, start it off right by beginning these exercises now. Happy traveling!

Be Cool, Calm, and Collected

Okay. *You've already* borne some or all of the insults of traffic and trains or airport lines and searches. You are now at the departure gate or platform. Your laptop and suitcases seem to weigh twice as much as they did when you started out. You suspiciously eye the woman with the two unruly children, hoping against hope that they will sit nowhere near you. And just for good measure, your flight will be delayed, uh, let's say two hours. (Am I right?)

It's time to regroup and center yourself. There is nothing you can do to change your circumstances—except to relax. You're there—whether at the gate or on the plane. Now's the time to spend a few moments healing from the trauma of your travels. Make the most of your time. You will find yourself more clearheaded and better able to carry on when you must. The exercises in this chapter were designed to calm you down and help you gather up what's left.

STEP ONE: **Drink Water**

Sit for a moment and collect yourself. Make yourself comfortable. Drink plenty of water to replenish and refresh. Remember, as you fly, you lose about two pints of water an hour. If the stewards tell you they have run out of water and you are out of your own stash, take the water reserved for hot tea. Cool it down a bit with some ice cubes. Water at room temperature is best, since water that is too cold can shock your intestines and interfere with warm digestive juices. And don't forget to spritz your face once in a while, too. Keep your environment moist.

Note: It is important to avoid imbibing alcoholic beverages while you attempt these exercises. Alcohol will impair your coordination and your ability to breathe properly.

STEP TWO: **Breathe**

Allow the thoughts and reverberating sounds of your trip to dissolve. Close your eyes; let your surroundings fade away. Follow your breath: focus on your chosen mantra or prayer. Inhale through your nose, then exhale through your mouth. Relax your facial muscles; relax your jaw; relax your shoulders. Check that your tongue is loose and not plastered to the roof of your mouth. As you breathe, gradually lengthen each inhalation and each exhalation. Remember to breathe deeply into your body: expanding your belly as you inhale, bringing your navel to your spine as you exhale. Don't allow your shoulders or your chest to rise and fall. Avoid tightening anywhere. Relax your hands on your knees; open your fingers. Relax your face; soften your brow. Allow your lips to be soft, not taut. Just breathe, long and deliciously. If you become dry, take some water, spritz your face, and moisturize your lips with balm.

STEP THREE: **Unload**

The following series of dynamic exercises was designed to help you unload and begin to prepare for the relaxation exercises described in Step Four. Start by becoming aware of your breath, counting "one" on the inhalation and "two" on the exhalation. Or you might want to use the mantra of your choice to reduce your awareness of the goings-on around you. When you are ready (remember, there is no race), follow the directions for the exercises and complete them in the prescribed order for the maximum benefit.

Shoulder Shrugs

The shoulders are often the first parts of the body to show problems; that is, we often wear our troubles like a burdensome yoke in the neck area, which becomes stiff and sore. This exercise will help you overcome the tension around your neck and shoulders.

Relax your shoulders and close your eyes. Rest your hands gently on your knees (if sitting) or at your sides (if standing). Become aware of your breath. After you have settled, keep your hands where they are, raise your shoulders to your ears, and inhale deeply

through your nostrils. Then drop your shoulders and exhale forcefully. Let the burdens fall off! Continue to inhale as you raise your shoulders; exhale as you lower them. Remember, there is no race. Move slowly.

Time: *One to three minutes*

Head Turns

Relax your brow, your jaw, and your shoulders. Breathe long and deeply for a few moments with your eyes closed. Begin to turn your head very slowly to the right and inhale as your chin reaches your right shoulder—eyes still closed. Very slowly, turn your head until your chin is over your left shoulder; then exhale. Continue inhaling as you

bring your chin to the right shoulder, exhaling as you bring it to the left shoulder. Move cautiously, slowly, smoothly. Don't force anything. Focus on your breath and your mantra. Continue to relax your face, your jaw, and your shoulders.

Time: *One to three minutes*

Head Rolls

Drop your head forward and bring your chin to your chest. Breathe long and deeply. Then gently roll your head around a full 360 degrees, sweeping your chin across your chest from shoulder to shoulder and then bringing your head up and around again. Inhale as you bring your head up; exhale as you drop it forward. Keep your shoulders relaxed as you move. Don't allow them to

hunch up toward your ears. If you experience neck or shoulder pain, move more slowly. Follow your breath. Relax into the movement. Continue in one direction for one minute, then head the other way.

Time: *One minute in each direction*

Infinity Rolls

Drop your head forward once again, bringing your chin to your chest. Grab your elbows with your hands and pull down slightly. Imagining your nose or chin as a pencil, "draw" the infinity symbol (a figure eight on its side) in the air. Breathe as you move your head through the air, keeping your eyes closed. Continue in one direction for one to two minutes, then reverse direction.

Time: *One to two minutes in each direction*

STEP FOUR: **Relax**

The exercises in this step can be practiced individually. Each was designed to bring you to a state of thought-free relaxation. By focusing on your breath and becoming aware of the rhythms of your body (for example, your pulse), you will eventually be able to slow your body down. Focusing on the breath and breathing consciously, long, and deeply has many benefits, including increasing the capacity of your lungs. In fact, it is nearly impossible to be angry when your breath is controlled and you are breathing long and deeply. Read through the following exercises, then try those that appeal to you.

Note: If you have a heart condition, please check with your physician before you attempt any of these exercises. Do not hold your breath out too long. Be sure to breathe gently and very slowly.

For Calmness

Sit comfortably with your feet flat on the floor, keeping your spine straight. You might wish to take your shoes off. (During commuter train rides home, I used to rest my feet on top of my shoes to avoid putting them directly on the floor.) Rest your left hand, palm up, on your left leg. Place the four fingers of your right hand (excluding the thumb) very gently onto your left wrist and find your pulse.

With your eyes closed, focus on your pulse. Follow the rhythm of your pulse; listen and breathe. Allow your breath to be gentle, soft, and long. Allow your eyes to roll up, still closed, but focused between your brows. If there is any tension anywhere in your body, allow it to dissipate. Relax your brow, your jaw, your tongue. As your pulse slows, your mind will follow.

Time: *Three to eleven minutes*

To Stop Unnerving Thoughts

Keeping your neck straight and
your head up, cast your eyes
down softly, allowing them
to remain open slightly. Make
a teepee with your hands.
Rest your elbows com-
fortably at your sides.
Let your pinkie
and ring fin-
gers fall away,
so that only your thumbs,
index, and middle fingers touch. Your thumbs
should point toward your body, the other fingers
away from your body. Now curve your index fingers so that the big knuckles (the second joints)
touch each other. Inhale and hold your breath for
as long as you comfortably can; exhale and hold
your breath out for as long as you comfortably can.
As you inhale and exhale, you can silently or softly
repeat your chosen mantra to center your mind on

your current task. Continue in this manner: inhale and hold, exhale and hold.

Time: *Three to eleven minutes*

Variation: Overcoming Negative Thoughts

Close your eyes and bring your hands to your heart center, palms together, as if in prayer. Relax your elbows at your sides. Push the fingers of your right hand against the fingers of your left hand (not the palm) and inhale. Hold this breath and continue pushing for a minute; exhale  and relax your fingers. Bring the disturbing thought to your mind. If the thought is still strong, push against your fingers again. Continue until the disturbing thought dissolves. Inhale as you push; hold the position and your breath; exhale as you relax your fingers.

Time: *Three to five minutes*

To Relieve Severe Tension

Tuck your chin into your neck. Keep your eyes slightly opened and focus your gaze downward without tilting your head forward. It is important that you keep your head straight. Bring your hands gently to your chest. Relax them on your breast with the fingers of each hand extended and pointed towards each other. Inhale for five seconds; completely exhale for five seconds; hold the breath out for fifteen seconds. Inhale and exhale while focusing your mind on your chosen mantra.

Time: *Three to eleven minutes*

For Deep Relaxation

Caution: Do not practice this one before a business meeting, before driving your car, or before any situation requiring an alert mind.

Relax your elbows at your sides. Make a fist with your right hand and cover the fist with the fingers of your left hand. Your thumbs should be resting parallel and against each other. Keep your neck back; do not drop your head forward. Allow your eyes to remain open slightly. Bring your hands to a point about four inches in front of your mouth. Inhale through your nose and exhale through your mouth, blowing gently through the little space between your thumbs. Continue breathing this way. This exercise is especially helpful when you are spending the night away from home.

Time: *Three to five minutes*

For Managing Tension

This is a good exercise for when you are too tense and must calm down immediately. Make a teepee with your hands—fingertips together, elbows resting comfortably at your sides, and hands near your heart. Inhale through your mouth and exhale through your nose. Breathe gently, long, and deeply. Continue with the breath, calming down further with each exhale. You may inhale on one and exhale on two, until you reach ten. Then start at one and begin again. Or you may use the mantra you have chosen. (During  a business meeting, you can just bring your fingertips together and breathe discreetly as described. You will maintain your composure and find that cool heads prevail.)

Time: *Three to five minutes*

Recharge Your Batteries

Traveling can leave you in a daze. Jet lag might have gotten the better of you or you might have fallen asleep in transit and, on awaking, felt less than bright. Just before landing or arriving at the station (or leaving your hotel room), you might need to recharge. If you are minutes away from giving a presentation, greeting a business associate, or having to find the right platform for the next leg of your trip, you need to be ready. When an alert mind is essential, try this set.

STEP ONE: **Raise Your Level of Energy**

The exercises in Step One constitute a set. They can also be used as preparatory exercises for any of the steps described in this book. Complete them in order and then choose one or more of the exercises described in Steps Two through Five. Use them to increase your energy and sharpen your mind.

Spinal Flex, Part One

Rest your hands gently on your knees (your feet should be flat on the floor). Now inhale deeply and press your chest forward, leaving your shoulders down and relaxed. Push your spine forward and your chest out as though someone were pinning a medal on your jacket. No tightness anywhere. On the exhale curve your spine back like a cat, leaving your shoulders in the same position as before. Continue inhaling as you flex forward, exhale as you arch back.

Time: *One to two minutes*

Spinal Flex, Part Two

Keeping both feet flat on the floor, lean as far forward as you can and bring your hands to your calves. Inhale and flex your chest forward with your head up; exhale and arch your back as in the previous exercise and drop your head forward. Continue, inhaling forward and exhaling back. Breathe long and deeply.

Time: *One to two minutes*

Massage and Pound

While you are still bending forward from Spinal Flex, Part Two, massage the back of your calves firmly and deeply. Come up slowly, make a fist with your hands, and begin pounding your thighs firmly. Be sure to pound your calves and also every spot on top of your thighs.

Keeping your hands in a fist, bring your hands behind you and pound on your butt. Be sure to get all the kinks out. Then gently pound the sides of your back where your kidneys are located. Move up and down along the kidneys. Continue pounding on your shoulders and the back of your neck.

Next, pound your chest. (Since it might be difficult to manage this discreetly, I suggest giving some explanation to your row partner beforehand!) Finally, pound your shoulders and neck. Breathe and beat.

Time: *One to two minutes, each area*

Head Rolls

Gently drop your head forward, and begin to roll it around your neck. With your eyes closed and rolled up, inhale as you bring your head back; exhale as you drop it forward. Bring your head back only as far as it will comfortably go. Be sure that your shoulders remain relaxed and not hunched as you move. Continue in one direction for a minute or so, then change direction.

Time: *One to two minutes*

Windmills

Grip the fingers of both hands together as illustrated. This is called "bear grip." Keep your hands at your heart center. Think of your hands as the center of a pinwheel. They should remain stationary. On the inhale, raise your left elbow; exhale and drop the left elbow and swing the right elbow up. Continue. Inhale and raise your left elbow and lower your right elbow; exhale and raise your right elbow and lower your left elbow. By keeping your hands at the heart center, there is no danger you will hit your neighbor with a flying elbow. Coordinate your movement with your breath and your mantra. Keep your eyes closed. Attempt to do this exercise vigorously, breathing strongly and deeply and moving your arms as quickly as you can.

Time: *One to two minutes*

Body Pumps

Interlace your fingers and bring them behind your neck, under any hair. Inhale deeply in the upright position; exhale as you lean as far forward as you comfortably can. Continue, inhaling up and exhaling down.

Time: *One to two minutes*

Body Drops

Make a fist with each of your hands and place them on the seat by your hips. (Note: Some people pre-fer pushing up on the palms of their hands, but this is not recommended if you have carpal tunnel syndrome or arthritis in your hands. Your fists will provide ample support.) Inhale and, pushing up with your fists, raise your body slightly off your seat; exhale and drop down.

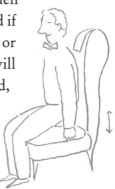

Time: *One minute*

STEP TWO: Energize Yourself with Right-Nostril Breathing

Long, deep breathing through the right nostril brings warmth and energy to the body. Wake up with long, deep breaths through your right nostril. (Before bed, try long, deep breathing through your left nostril for a tranquilizing effect.)

Lightly press against your left nostril with your index finger or thumb. Begin to breathe long and deeply through your right nostril. Keep your eyes closed throughout. Attempt to lengthen your inhalations and exhalations with each breath.

Time: *Three to five minutes*

STEP THREE: **Sharpen Your Wits**

Rest your left arm at your side and raise your left palm as though you were going to clap it against your right hand. You may rest the side of your hand against your chest or keep it at a height that is comfortable for you. With your right hand, allow your index and middle fingers to walk slowly up the center of your left palm to the tips of your middle and ring fingers. When you reach the tips of your fingers, start all over again. While you are doing this, keep your eyes opened slightly and focused on the tip of your  nose. Continue walking your fingers. Be mindful of your breath, and keep it slow, long, and even. You need not coordinate this movement with your inhale or exhale.

Time: *Two to three minutes*

STEP FOUR: **Enhance Confidence**

This exercise is especially effective before you make a presentation at a meeting or when you must appear confident.

Recharge, Part One

Bring your hands together at the pinkies, keeping your palms up. Allow your elbows to remain relaxed at your sides. With your eyes opened slightly and softly focused on your palms, 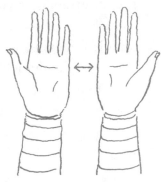 bring the sides of your hands together. Palms up, eyes downcast, clap the sides of your hands back and forth rapidly against each other. Breathe long and deeply through your nostrils as you begin. About two minutes into the exercise, begin to breathe through your mouth for another two or three minutes.

Time: *Three to five minutes*

Recharge, Part Two

When you have finished Part One, bring your hands to your chest and make a fist with your right hand. Wrap your left hand around your right fist, bringing the sides of your thumbs together. Your

thumbs should be
parallel to each
other. In this posi-
tion, inhale slowly through
your nostrils (five seconds); exhale
slowly through your nostrils (five seconds) so that
your breath skims your thumbs; hold your breath
out for fifteen seconds. Continue in this manner.

Time: *Three to five minutes*

Note: If you have a heart condition, do not attempt
to hold your breath out for an extended length of
time unless you have first consulted your physician. Instead, try this variation: Bring your arms
into the same position described above. Inhale
slowly through your nose; exhale slowly through
your mouth. Pucker your mouth as you exhale, as
if you're blowing a silent whistle.

STEP FIVE: Command Your Voice

If you must give a presentation or speak in a large
room full of people, you must have a commanding

presence and voice. To prepare, practice the following exercise. You might wish to do this in the privacy of your rental car or room since it does require chanting aloud and loudly.

Bring your hands to your throat, palms up. Allow your extended fingers to act as a bullhorn, throwing the sound forward. Inhale long and deeply until your lungs are full. Chant the sound *tho* loudly and firmly for as long as you can. When you must, take another breath, then chant the sound *tho* once again. Do this several times, until your voice has freed up and you feel the sound is powerful and will project well as you speak in a room full of people.

3

Relieve Stiff Muscles, Aches, and Pains

eadache, stiffness, general aches and pains? Not enough sleep the night before? Last-minute packing? Eyes sore from working through the night in preparation for an important business meeting? Try this set and undo the damage! Each step in this chapter has merit in itself and can be practiced alone. Each can also be practiced in sequence. In time, you will discover which one(s) will best suit your needs.

STEP ONE: **Rest Your Eyes Right**

These exercises will help cleanse your corneas of toxins and help you overcome eyestrain and fatigue. You also might want to try these eye exercises as  you relax in a salt bath (as described in Chapter 7). Practice the exercises in Step One as a complete set.

Note: Remove contact lenses before starting these exercises.

1. Stare softly at an object with one eye. Try not to blink, and allow your eye to tear. This helps clear toxins from the surface of the eye.

Time: *One minute for each eye; repeat as necessary*

2. Sit with your spine straight and pull in your chin. Keep your head erect. Bring your forefinger

to a point about six inches from your nose and allow your eyes to focus on it. Now, focus on a spot at the farthest end of the room (or plane or train, et cetera) and once again, focus your gaze. Alternate your gaze between your finger and the far corner you have selected. Move your eyes only after you have focused them.

Time: *One minute*

3. Begin to move your eyes in a circle, first clockwise, then counterclockwise. Move your eyes as far as you can in all directions. Remember to breathe as you roll your eyes. Moving your eyes clockwise

and counterclockwise stretches and strengthens the ocular muscles. It might feel uncomfortable at first, but the benefits are amazing.

Time: *One minute in each direction; repeat as necessary*

4. Without moving your head (keep your chin tucked), look up as far as you possibly can, then look down. Do this about ten times. Still keeping your head straight ahead, direct your gaze to the

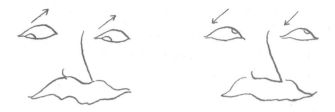

upper right corner of the room, then to the lower left corner. Do this ten times. Now direct your gaze from the upper left corner of the room to the lower right corner. Do this ten times.

Time: *Open*

5. Now close your eyes and attempt to focus them at the back of your head (didn't you used to say your mom had eyes in the back of her head?). Just sit still and focus and breathe.

Time: *Two minutes*

6. Sitting with your spine straight, tilt your head back just a little. Open your eyes wide and stare at

a spot on the ceiling. Allow your eyes to remain open until they tear. This will help cleanse impurities from your eyes.

Time: *Two minutes*

STEP TWO: **Get Ahead of the Game**

If you have been scattered all day and somewhat headachy, try this posture. This exercise will help center you.

Bring your left palm to your forehead (fingers pointing toward the right) and your right palm to the back of your neck (fingers pointing toward the left). Sit in this posture with your spine straight and your feet flat on the floor and breathe

long and deeply. Keep your eyes closed and focused at your brow; feel good.

Time: *Open*

STEP THREE: **Strengthen Your Nerves of Steel**

This exercise will prepare you for anything, including hours of desk work. Concentrate and coordinate your breath with the movements, gradually increasing your speed.

1. Rest your hands on your knees, palms up. Curl your fingers in toward the pads of your hands, but stretch your thumbs away from your hands. On the inhale, stretch your thumbs out further. On the exhale, curl your thumbs in. Continue, coordinating the movement of your thumbs

with your breath. Close your eyes and focus on your breath. Gradually pick up your speed until you are moving your thumbs quickly.

Time: *One to two minutes*

2. Make a fist of each hand, thumbs inside. With your elbows resting against your sides, gently rotate your hands in tight circles. Breathe long and deeply as you move your fists, first outward, then inward. Keep your eyes closed. Relax.

Time: *One minute in each direction*

3. Now stretch your fingers fully. Your elbows are still at your sides. Gently rotate your hands in circles from your wrists: first inward, then outward. These two

exercises work wonders on mild carpal tunnel problems.

Time: *One minute in each direction*

STEP FOUR: **Boost Your Immune System**

This exercise is particularly beneficial if practiced daily upon rising. It will cool your head and refresh your mouth. Do it twenty-six times (in other words, take twenty-six breaths) before you begin your day, and see what a difference it makes. Try it if you have just awakened from a nap on the train or plane.

Sit with your spine straight and your hands resting on your knees. Curl your tongue into a U-shape and allow it to protrude beyond your lips. (Note: The ability to curl your tongue is genetic. If you cannot curl it, just protrude your tongue slightly beyond your lips.) Inhale deeply through your mouth as though sipping through a straw; exhale through your nose. Continue in this manner with your eyes closed. Do not rush through this exercise.

Time: *Two to three minutes*

STEP FIVE: **Build Stamina**

Bring your hands to your knees, palms up. Inhale deeply through your nostrils and hold your breath in. With the breath held in, sequentially press your thumbs against your index, middle, ring, and little fingers. (The thumb of the right hand presses the tips of the fingers of the right hand; thumb of the left hand presses the tips of the fingers of the left hand.) Continue moving your thumbs to the tips

of your fingers in the same order with the breath held in. Exhale when you need to take a breath, then inhale and continue the sequence.

Time: *Two to three minutes*

STEP SIX: **Regenerate**

With your feet flat on the floor, your spine straight, and your eyes closed, fold your arms gently across your chest. Relax your shoulders and drop your head back slightly. Breathe long and deeply through your nostrils.

Time: *Open*

4

Loosen Tightness in Your Head and Neck

Traveling can make your muscles tighten up. Let's say the shuttle bus didn't stop for you and you wound up parking in Long-Term Parking Z, a mere fifteen miles from the airport. But you made the flight (or the next flight), and now your neck and back are punishing you for running through the airport pulling twenty pounds of luggage (or computer equipment). Your body now needs major repairs to loosen you up for the rest of the trip. The following exercises work mainly on your head, neck, shoulders, and back. Your body will thank you for the attention.

STEP ONE: **Roll Your Head**

With your eyes closed, drop your head forward and bring your chin to your chest. Relax your brow, your jaw, and your shoulders. Check to see that your tongue is resting loosely in your mouth. Begin to rotate your head around your neck. As you gently rotate it toward the back (but not too far back), inhale. As you rotate it forward, exhale. Be sure that you bring your ears to your shoulders as you rotate. Relax into the movement. Continue very slowly in one direction for a minute or two, then reverse course.

Time: *One to three minutes*

STEP TWO: **Loosen Your Jaw**

With your eyes still closed, open your mouth as wide as possible. Bring your right ear to your right shoulder. You will feel some pulling if your neck is tight. Move cautiously. Next, bring your left ear to your left shoulder with your mouth still opened wide. Continue very slowly moving your head from shoulder to shoulder. To intensify this exercise, place your left hand on the crown of your head when your head is tilted toward your left shoulder; when your head is tilted toward your right shoulder, place your right hand on your crown.

Time: *One to two minutes*

STEP THREE: **Adjust Your Face and Neck**

Until you do the following exercises, you won't realize how tight your facial and neck muscles have become. These exercises will loosen your jaw muscles and relieve tightness around your neck and shoulders. Practice the exercises in Step Three as a complete set.

1. Jut your jaw forward in an exaggerated underbite. Bare your upper teeth, and wrinkle your nose. Focus your eyes on your nose. (You might not want to try this when the flight attendant or train conductor is likely to walk by.) Rest your hands gently on your knees. Raise your shoulders to your ears. Breathe long and deeply, and maintain this winning expression.

Time: *Two minutes*

2. Bring the heels of your hands to your temples and gently rest your fingers on your head. Inhale

and twist your upper body to the right; exhale and twist your upper body to the left. Continue inhaling as you twist to the right and exhaling as you twist to the left. Relax your facial muscles and shoulders as you move.

Time: *One to two minutes*

STEP FOUR: **Adjust Your Neck, Part Two**

Place the palm of your right hand against the right side of your neck. Keep your fingers pointing toward the back of your neck. Now, place the palm of your left hand against your left temple. Keep the fingers of both hands pointing toward the back of

your head. Relax your facial muscles, your jaw, and your tongue. Gently push your hands and resist with your neck muscles.

Time: *One minute*

STEP FIVE: **Massage Your Face**

The following exercises will relieve facial muscle tension and minor sinus congestion you might not even be aware of. Hold the described positions so that you feel significant pressure. Practice the exercises in Step Five as a complete set.

1. Bring your fingers to the crown of your head and place your thumbs in the cavity just under your cheekbones. Press your thumbs against the cavity with some force  and massage the area. There might be some discomfort. Work through it—just sit and breathe and massage.

Time: *One to two minutes*

2. Bring the heels of your hands under your cheekbones and push hard. Rest your fingers on your head. This might not hurt, but then again,

it might. In any case, you will find that it relieves tension superbly. Keep your eyes closed and your jaw relaxed. Breathe long and deeply. Allow your shoulders to relax.

Time: *One to three minutes*

3. Bring the first three fingers of each hand to the top of your cheekbones, just under your eyes. Massage this area by rotating both hands in toward your nose for a minute or so. Then massage in the other direction, away from your nose. Gently but rapidly, massage your cheekbones.

Time: *Two to five minutes*

4. With your eyes closed and hands relaxed on your knees, roll your tongue over your teeth and

gums. This gives the jaw and tongue a great workout.

Time: *One to two minutes*

STEP SIX: **Rotate Your Shoulders**

Relax your hands on your knees. Don't grip with your fingers. Your head should be erect and aligned with your spine; close your eyes and tuck in your chin. Gently rotate your shoulders in forward circles for one minute, then backward for one minute, breathing deeply as you move.

Time: *One minute in each direction*

STEP SEVEN: **Rest Your Back**

Keeping limber on a long trip is your only defense against pain upon rising. Stretching your back muscles will prevent undue stiffness and a possible pulled muscle when you attempt to retrieve your luggage from the top rack. Complete the following two exercises as a set.

1. Grasp opposite elbows with your hands. Your feet should be flat on the floor and your spine should be straight. Close your eyes. As you inhale, raise your crossed arms as high as you possibly can. On the exhale, lower them. Continue raising and lowering your crossed arms as rapidly as you can, coordinating this movement with your breath.

Time: *One minute*

2. Grasp opposite elbows behind your back and continue the same movement, raising your arms as far as you comfortably can (this might only be an inch or two) on the inhale and lowering them on the exhale. You might find that your shoulders need the extra attention. If you cannot attain any movement while grasping your elbows, modify the movement by grasping your wrists. It will be just as effective.

Time: *One minute*

STEP EIGHT:
Arch Your Spine

Lock your wrists behind your back and pull down. Arch your spine forward. In this posture, breathe long and deeply. Close

your eyes and be sure to keep your chin tucked. You'll find your energy and your spirits raised.

Time: *One to three minutes*

STEP NINE: **Rotate Your Back**

Grasp opposite shoulders with your hands and begin to swing your body freely and loosely from right to left from your waist, inhaling as you turn your torso to the left and exhaling as you turn it to the right. As you twist to the right, bring your chin to your right shoulder. As you twist to the left, bring your chin to your left shoulder.

Time: *One minute*

STEP TEN: **Take a Rest and Give Yourself a Hug**

Continue to hold opposite shoulders with your hands. Close your eyes, and drop your head forward and relax. Breathe long and deeply. Relax.

Time: *Open*

5

Fight the Cooped-Up Feeling: Move!

When you're traveling, there are times when you feel you have to either move or burst. Being captive in a car, airplane, bus, or train for a long time can be excruciating. The exercises in this chapter are designed to increase your vitality and stamina as you travel, and to get the kinks out.

Whenever you can, get up and walk around. Being immobile for an extended period of time has been known to cause blood clots in the legs. So movement is important. By the way, if you drink lots of water, getting up to use the facilities from time to time won't hurt.

STEP ONE: Strengthen Your Back

While sitting, interlace your fingers and bring your hands behind your neck, under any hair. Inhale in the upright position, then exhale, and bending at the waist, bring your right elbow to your left knee. Inhale up again, then exhale down, bringing your left elbow to the right knee. Continue in this manner—inhaling up and exhaling down to your opposite knee.

Time: *One to two minutes*

STEP TWO: "Tenderize" Your Muscles

Extend your left arm in front of your chest with your palm up. Make a fist with your right hand and begin to pound your left arm from elbow to wrist. Then switch arms. Continue in the same manner, pounding your right arm with your left fist.

Time: *One minute for each arm*

STEP THREE: Flex Your Spine

With your hands resting gently on your knees, flex your back forward on the inhale and arch back like a cat on the exhale. Continue flexing your back in the same manner, but after a minute, bring your hands to your hips. On the inhale, as you arch your back for- ward, bring your elbows as far back as you comfortably can. On the exhale, as you arch back, flap your elbows forward. Continue in this manner.

Time: *One minute with hands on your knees and one minute with hands on your hips*

STEP FOUR: **Rotate Your Shoulders**

Relax your hands on your knees or let them flop loosely at your sides. Your head should be erect and aligned with your spine. Don't forget to keep your eyes closed and your chin tucked. Gently rotate your shoulders in forward circles for one minute, then in backward circles for one minute, breathing deeply as you move.

Time: *One minute in each direction*

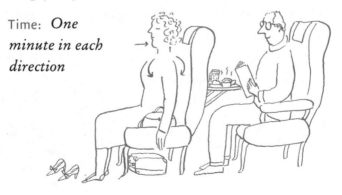

STEP FIVE: **Swing Your Arms**

When you really need to get the kinks out of your shoulders and your upper back, this set is the way to go. Try these three exercises in order, moving strongly and breathing deeply. Eventually, you will get to a point where you hear only your breathing.

1. With your hands in fists (thumbs inside), swing your arms forcefully across your chest—right arm to the left and left arm to the right *simultaneously*. (Be careful not to sock your neighbor in the head or face.) Alternate right arm over left, then left arm over right. You should feel this in your shoulders and upper back. It's great for the neck, too.

Attempt to coordinate your breath with the movement. Inhale strongly with the first swing and exhale with the second. This breathing pattern will help you overcome anger or resentment.

Or you can inhale and exhale with the first swing and inhale and exhale with the second, and so on. This breathing pattern will quicken your pulse and energize you.

Time: *One to two minutes*

2. With the same motion, bring both arms overhead simultaneously and cross them over the crown of your head. Alternate right arm in front, then left arm in front.

Time: *One minute*

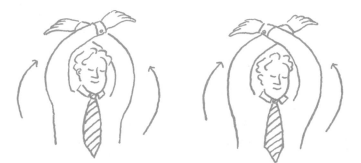

3. Repeat the first part of the exercise, swinging both arms across your chest.

Time: *One minute*

STEP SIX: Roll Your Head

With your eyes closed, drop your head forward. Relax your hands on your knees and keep your shoulders down. Move your head slowly and carefully around your neck. Inhale as you bring it up; exhale as you drop it forward. Change direction after one minute and head the other way.

Time: *One minute each direction*

STEP SEVEN: Move Your Nimble Fingers

With your hands in your lap, make fists, leaving your thumbs inside. Then open your hands and make fists with your thumbs outside. Rapidly make fists, alternating with thumbs inside, then outside.

Coordinate your breath with your movements. Inhale and move your thumbs in and out four times. Then exhale and move your thumbs in and out of your fists four more times.

Time: *Two minutes*

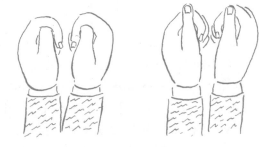

STEP EIGHT: Awaken Your Feet

If you have been sitting for a long time, chances are your feet are swollen. If you have taken your shoes off, putting them back on might be somewhat challenging. Although this exercise will not reduce the swelling entirely, it will help stimulate the circulation in your lower extremities.

1. With your heels on the floor, rotate your feet in circles away from each other. Then reverse direc-

tion and rotate them toward each other.

Time: *One to two minutes in each direction*

2. Keeping your heels on the floor, flap your feet up and down slowly, giving your calves a good stretch as you move. If you wish, you can put a book under your feet and place your heels at the far edge of the book. Doing this will allow you to lower your toes and stretch the tendons on the top side of your feet when you flap your feet forward.

Time: *One to two minutes*

STEP NINE: **Relax**

Choose one of the relaxation exercises described in Chapter 1, Step Four.

6

Overcome Travel Rage

s life, *your spouse, the client,* the airline, or the travel service demanding the impossible of you and delivering less than you'd hoped? Plane or train delayed or canceled? Important business deal fallen through? Collect yourself and follow these instructions. Remember, your mind will obey the rate of your breath. Attempt to slow your breathing. Take a long drink of cool water. You might also need to drink some water between the following exercises.

STEP ONE: Breathe Through Your Left Nostril

With your feet flat on the floor, your spine straight, and your eyes closed, follow your breath. Pay attention to the sound of your breathing. Allow your breath to slow down. Then close off your right nostril and begin to breathe long and deeply from your left nostril. Doing this will cool your body and help calm you down. If you are especially hotheaded, you might want to make this a regular practice and increase the amount of water you drink each day. Remember, the left side of the body is the cool side. (For an energizing breath, breathe long and deeply from your right nostril.)

Time: *Two to five minutes*

STEP TWO: Alternate-Nostril Breathing

1. Close off your right nostril with your right thumb, and inhale through your left nostril. Then

close off your left nostril with your pinkie and exhale through the right nostril. Continue in this manner. Breathe long and deeply.

Time: *One to two minutes*

2. Now reverse the breath. Inhale through the right nostril and exhale through the left. Take long, deep breaths.

Time: *One to two minutes*

STEP THREE: Eliminate Pent-Up Anger

Make fists with your hands, thumbs inside. Inhale deeply. Hold your breath and thrust your arms out in front as though you are shadowboxing. Keep your eyes closed and continue punching until you must exhale. Then inhale and hold the breath again and resume punching.

Time: *One to two minutes*

STEP FOUR: Pound Your Chest

With your hands in fists, begin to pound your chest. (Ever seen a Tarzan movie or caught Carol Burnett in one of her amazing demonstrations?) Keep your feet flat on the floor and your eyes closed. Pound firmly and breathe deeply.

Time: *One to two minutes*

STEP FIVE: Engage in Imaginary Pulls

Make your hands into fists and stretch them out in front; inhale deeply and hold your breath. With the breath held in, bring your hands slowly to your chest as though you were pulling a 100-pound

weight. When your hands reach your chest, exhale and extend your arms once again. Repeat this exercise only twice more.

Time: *Three repetitions only*

STEP SIX: Practice Navel Pumps

Let's face it, traveling is tough work and requires strength of body and mind. People will be less likely to challenge you or take advantage of you when they sense you are strong. Practitioners of Tai Chi and yoga call the area at and below the navel the "seat of power." This exercise will help strengthen that power area so you can stay strong while on the road. It is best done on an empty stomach.

Rest your hands on your knees, palms up. Follow your breath until it is slow and deep. Then inhale deeply and exhale completely. With the breath held out, pump your navel. To do this, just bring your navel to your spine (by contracting your abdominal muscles), then relax. With your breath held out, attempt to pump your navel three to six times: contract, relax; contract, relax; contract, relax; et cetera. Then inhale and completely exhale again, and then pump your navel. Continue inhaling, exhaling, then pumping your navel for as long as you can on one breath.

Time: *One to three minutes*

STEP SEVEN: Scratch Your Back

With your right hand resting on your right knee, bring your left hand to your right shoulder blade at your back. Your palm should be facing out and your fingers should be pointing toward the sky. Reach as far as you can comfortably. In this posture, inhale deeply and then exhale. With your breath held out, squeeze the muscles in the lower triangle of your body: rectum, genitals, and navel. Squeeze these muscles for as long as you can. When you must take a breath, relax and begin the cycle again. Inhale, squeeze up, and exhale. There is no need to switch hands with this exercise.

Time: *One to three minutes*

STEP EIGHT: **Squeeze Your Body**

Fold your arms across your body and place your hands under your armpits with your palms flat against your body. Drop your head onto your chest, close your eyes, and raise your shoulders up toward your ears as far as they will

THE STRESS-FREE TRAVELER

go. Breathe long and deeply. Keep your eyes closed and squeeze your hands against your body. Focus on your breath.

Time: *Three to eleven minutes*

STEP NINE: **Relax**

Just sit with your eyes closed and relax. Rest your hands on your knees, palms up, and allow the sounds around you to dissolve.

Time: *Open*

7

Unwind and Repair at the End of Your Journey

Y ou have finally made it. Either you're at the
hotel or back at home-sweetest-home, attaché
case or suitcase safely tucked away. If you
have time before you must go off to a meeting or
do the sights, do yourself a favor and try any of the
steps recommended in this chapter. Don't wait
until you are desperate. Treat yourself anytime:
after you pack the children off to school or your
spouse to the airport; after a difficult day at the
office; after a great day at the office; before you

embark on another journey; when you arrive at your destination; or when you return home. Just remember one rule: pamper yourself!

STEP ONE: **Take a Salt Bath**

After rushing to get to the airport terminal or train station or whatever and then sitting in an enclosed and restricted space for however many hours, you are probably not feeling very fresh. Remember, the air you breathed and shared with so many people, including the fellow who coughed and sneezed constantly behind you, wasn't very pure. Time for a cleansing bath—the kind that draws impurities from the body and washes away a day's worth of grime and perspiration. Time to refresh.

When you can't make it to the spa, create one for yourself. Draw a warm bath and fill the tub with a cup of kosher salt or sea salt. Dead Sea salts, available at many health food stores, will draw impurities from your skin. Set the mood for relaxation: if you have access to a portable tape or CD player or an iPod, put on your favorite music while you soak. (Be sure to keep the equipment away from the water!) Try turning off the lights. Sitting in a warm tub with no light can help you overcome the assault on your senses rendered by travel and your hectic routine.

You can purchase bath pillows and backrests for these moments, too. Otherwise, just roll up a towel and rest it under your neck. Now sit back and relax for about twenty minutes. After your soak, massage your body with a loofah or a washcloth. Soap down as usual and rinse off in a cool shower to

tighten your skin and minimize your pores. A cool shower won't awaken you at the end of the day, and it might provide a more restful sleep. You will be surprised how good this feels after a warm salt bath.

While in the shower, turn your back to the water. Bring your hands to your elbows, and allow the water to massage your neck. Grasp your elbows and pull down slightly. Get rid of those final kinks in your neck.

When you leave the shower, massage yourself vigorously with the towel. Then firmly massage your body with pure almond oil—the highest quality you can find. (If you don't happen to have almond oil, use your favorite lotion or even the hotel lotion.) You can run the bottle of oil or lotion under warm water for a few minutes before you

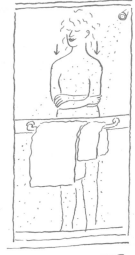

apply it. The warm oil will be very soothing and will penetrate your skin more easily. Apply oils or lotions immediately after toweling (within two minutes is best) to ensure maximal absorption into your skin. Be sure to wipe off any excess oil so that your clothing will not become stained.

STEP TWO: **Give Yourself an Almond Oil Foot Massage**

When you are on the road, your feet can take a beating and may demand extra attention. Prop yourself up on the bed or on a comfortable chair. With a towel under your feet to absorb excess oil, pour some of the almond oil into your hands and massage your feet. Carefully massage each toe, the sides of your feet, your heels, and the balls of your feet. If you find any knots in your feet, use your knuckles to work them out. Rub your hands along the sides of your feet. Making a fist, work your knuckles up and down the soles of your feet. When your feet begin to tingle or when you have mas-

saged every area, wrap them in the towel and rest
a bit more.

STEP THREE: Engage in Left-Nostril Breathing

You are finally ready for bed and want to be sure
to have a decent night's sleep before your first day
of vacation or meetings. Time for total relaxation.
Left-nostril breathing will start you on your way.
Cover your right nostril with your right thumb.
With your spine straight, your eyes closed, and
your chin tucked slightly, breathe long and deeply

from your left nostril. Relax your shoulders and your chest.

Time: *Three to five minutes*

STEP FOUR: **Flex Your Spine**

It's always a good idea to loosen up the spine before or after activities as well as at the beginning and end of your day. Keeping your spine flexible will help prevent backaches, especially upon rising in the morning (if it doesn't, your mattress might need replacing). A flexible spine is highly prized because energy rises up from the base of your spine to the crown of your head. Blocked energy from an inflexible spine can cause many problems, not the least of which is low energy.

Rest your hands gently on your knees. Inhale deeply and fully and hold the breath in. With the breath held in, quickly press your chest forward, then arch back like a cat, keeping your chin parallel to the ground. Move forward and back without leaking any air from your lungs, until you must exhale. Continue in this manner—inhaling and holding the breath and moving your spine quickly forward and back for as long as you can. When you must, exhale and start all over.

Time: *Five to eleven minutes*

STEP FIVE: Give Yourself a Jet Lag Fix

Presumably, you have just traveled many miles from home and are now about to rest in an area with a different electromagnetic field—that is, an energy quite different from what your body is accustomed to. If you arrived by plane, you rode for a while in another electromagnetic field several miles above the earth. Your body needs to shake the electrical "confusion." The salt bath will have helped some, but this exercise will be the icing on the cake. Try it: you will want to make this exercise a permanent part of your travel agenda.

Sitting up straight in your chair with feet flat on the floor or sitting on the floor with your legs crossed, rest your hands in your lap. With your palms up, place your right hand on top of your left hand and allow the tips of your thumbs to touch, pointing away from your body.

Your eyes should be half opened, looking down toward your nose. Through your nostrils, inhale, taking in four long deep breaths until your lungs are filled. Hold your breath in for sixteen seconds, equivalent to the length of each inhale you took. Then exhale in two parts. Contine this pattern.

Time: *Five to thirty-one minutes. Gradually lengthen the time by adding a minute or two to each practice.*

STEP SIX: Drink Warm Milk and Honey

Chances are your throat is dry, particularly if you have flown for any distance. Water helps, but honey soothes. There is nothing worse than being unable to sleep because of a tickle in your throat. And it your room is not especially hypoallergenic, your allergies might kick up. Honey, especially local honey, can help you overcome pollen-associated allergies by giving you a sort of "hair of the dog that is biting you." And it has a natural antibacterial effect! If you're at a hotel, ring room service and have them bring up some warm milk and honey. If you are allergic to cow's milk, there are some wonderful substitutes, such as rice milk or soy milk, which come packed conveniently in cartons perfect for travel. If you prefer, take green tea or herbal tea—but don't forget the honey.

8

Refresh: Get Ready to Face a New Day

f you were unable to prepare properly for a good night's sleep, or your room was too close to the elevator or a room full of college seniors celebrating the end of session, you probably had a restless sleep or no sleep at all. Sleeping away from home sometimes takes getting used to. Some people even bring their own pillows or pillowcases to help them acclimate to the new room more quickly. But now, the morning after, it might be time to meet your associate for an early breakfast to review the details of the 8:30 A.M. conference with potential clients or the 8:30 A.M. walk over hot coals with current clients. On the other hand, you might be ready to take in the sights or the pool. To make the most of this day, prepare for it wisely.

STEP ONE: **Start Recharging**

Choose any of the exercises described in Chapter 2.

STEP TWO: **Try Cross-Crawls**

If you feel particularly out of sorts, these exercises will be the ticket. They will balance the right and left hemispheres of your brain and prevent you from being scattered. If you keep dropping things or can't remember where (or if) you packed (or unpacked) your socks, if you have to check to see where those darned room keys are for the tenth time, or if you have to check your Palm Pilot for the twentieth time for the meeting place and date, take the time to unravel the mental mess with these exercises before you leave the room. These exercises will also benefit your eyes. I found that after several weeks of practicing them daily, my eyes were less sore and focused more easily. But maintaining the advantage requires continual practice. These exercises should be practiced as a set; however, if you find you don't have time for all of them, then try at least three. Make them a part of your daily routine. Attempt to coordinate your breath as you move.

Supine Synchronizer

Lying on your back, inhale and simultaneously raise your right leg and left arm so they are per-

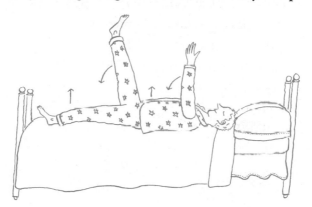

pendicular to your body. Exhale and lower them. Now, inhale and raise your left leg and right arm. Then exhale and lower them. Continue in this manner, raising opposite arms and legs as you inhale and lowering them as you exhale.

Note: To benefit your eyes, you can keep your eyes open while you do this. First get used to the rhythm of the movement. Then rotate your eyes counterclockwise for one minute and clockwise for one minute.

Time: *One to two minutes*

Abdomen Strengthener Cross-Crawl

Remember that the abdomen is the "seat of power." It pays to have a strong abdomen. Remain on your back and intertwine your fingers behind your neck under any hair. On the inhale, bring your right elbow to your left knee, raising your left knee toward your head. Exhale and lower your head and your knee. Next, inhale and bring your left elbow to your right knee in the same manner. Continue at a pace comfortable for you. This is great for the abdomen! (You can keep your eyes closed for this exercise. But remember to coordinate your breath with the movement.)

Time: *One to two minutes*

Stretch that Hip: Cat/Cow Cross-Crawl

Get onto your hands and knees. Keep your knees about hip-width apart. Your hands should be on the floor just under your shoulders. On the inhale, raise your right arm and left leg. Exhale and bring them down. Inhale again and raise your left arm

and right leg. Exhale and lower them. Continue inhaling while moving up with the opposite arm and leg and exhaling while lowering them.

Time: *One to two minutes*

Standing Series of Cross-Crawls

The standing cross-crawls require that you keep your eyes open. To begin, you can focus your eyes on an object on the opposite wall, but keep your head erect. As you become accustomed to the exercises, you might wish to try rotating your eyes clockwise (for one minute or more) and then counterclockwise (for one minute or more) as you complete the movement.

1. Standing erect, swing both arms to the left across your body and bring your left knee to the right side, across the center line of your torso. Coordinate your breath with your movements and continue alternating right and left.

Time: *One to two minutes*

2. Still standing, bring your right hand behind your neck and your left hand to your right ankle in front of your body. Then place your left hand behind your neck and bring your right hand to your left ankle. Continue these movements, alternating right and left. Coordinate your breath with your movements.

Time: *One to two minutes*

3. Still standing, bring your right hand to your left ankle behind you. Swing your left arm across your body in front. Continue with this same movement on the other side. Again, coordinate your breath with each movement.

Time: *One to two minutes*

STEP THREE: **Breathe**

Follow these with any of the breathing exercises in this book (see pages 49 and 92). Take at least eleven minutes. You will have all day for touring or negotiating. Start your day strongly for a good finish.

And remember: don't take any of this or any of what happens to you in your travels too seriously. Above all, enjoy yourself!